D1220055

First published in 2002

Allen & Unwin
83 Alexander St
Crows Nest NSW 2065
Australia
Phone: (61 2) 8425 0100
Fax: (61 2) 9906 2218
Email: info@allenandunwin.com
Web: www.allenandunwin.com

National Library of Australia
Cataloguing-in-Publication entry:
Paul, Anthea.

         Girlosophy: the oracle.

         ISBN 1 86508 819 6.
         1. Self-perception in women 2. Self-esteem in women.
         3. Self actualization (Psychology) I. Title.

158.1082

Concept by Anthea Paul
Art Direction and Design by Justine O'Donnell for jmedia design, Sydney, Australia
Cover Photography by Ashley de Prazer
Illustration by Sally Prisk
Printed in Singapore by Imago Productions (F.E.) PTE. LTD

10 9 8 7 6 5 4 3 2 1

girlosophy

THE ORACLE

Anthea Paul

ALLEN&UNWIN

C o n t

ents

Introduction

ASK THE UNIVERSE + OPEN *THE ORACLE* = GET THE MESSAGE!

Welcome to *girlosophy—The Oracle*! If it's questions you have and answers you need, then you'll find they're all covered here. This is your go-to guide and one-stop-shop reference on one of the Universe's deepest mysteries: YOU! Within these pages you'll find all the support you require and, hopefully, a good many flashes of inspiration to get you into your day or over whatever hump you may be facing.

It's all a question of timing, and the aim of this book is to help you to be "in tune" and "on time" so that your life flows smoothly in all areas.

As a girlosopher you know that being independent is where it's at and therefore anything that helps you to be autonomous and more in control of your life is worth investigating. Put it this way, receiving another piece of the puzzle always helps, don't you think? And that's where *The Oracle* comes in.

WHY *THE ORACLE*?

In the past when I've had decisions to make or situations to solve, I've often found I need what I call a "link," which is a kind of bridge between one decision, action or reaction and another. For me, a link is that mid-point connection between myself and the Universe, or what I call the Infinite Intelligence, which points me in the direction that is for my highest good—my personal destiny.

A "link" can be the taxi driver who is driving you to the airport (they can be excellent for objective advice!) or that favorite and unbiased aunt or godmother who knows you well. Sometimes I'll be in a car and see a numberplate or a billboard that gives me a word or phrase which seems to directly relate to something I've been pondering or dealing with. If it helps me to gain some clarity, then for me that's a link. Other times I'll pick up a magazine or a newspaper and find an article that concerns something I've been recently thinking about or I flip randomly to a feature profile on a person whose quotes offer advice that is relevant to me at the time. These are also links. Links are some of the infinite ways we receive information and messages from beyond, for the Universe truly works in mysterious and magical ways.

You can receive messages from any number of sources. You just have to be aware of your surroundings and stay "on it" to clue in and get the help—or the vibe—you need. But sometimes you're stuck in a room at say, school or the office, where there is no outside solution in sight. That's when having a definitive source of links nearby, such as *The Oracle*, is so useful.

WHAT IS *THE ORACLE*?

Often I'm tackling a pressing issue and I've needed another (higher) perspective to help me think it through or to give me the motivation I need to do something about it. And rather than bugging my best friend or my mother with endless "*What should I do*?!" phone calls and stretching the relationship, I prefer to consult a neutral sounding board so I can try and figure it out for myself. And that's what an oracle is and does: it's a sounding board between you and the Universe, and its purpose is to key you into what you need to hear or do.

As always, free will is the cornerstone of anyone's experience and you alone are ultimately responsible for making (or not making!) the move or thinking the thought. You're in the driver's seat of your own life and what you do with the information you receive from *The Oracle*—or any other source for that matter—is up to you. It's not about surrendering your highest wisdom or instinct to an outside force. In fact, it's quite the opposite: it's all about heightening your awareness and using your intuition to increase your independence. By working with higher energies you will better be able to maximize your situation. *The Oracle* is the link between you and the highest intelligence source available: the Universe. To be wise is to be "with knowledge," and having knowledge gives you the edge in any situation.

WHAT'S IN *THE ORACLE*?

Time to get down to the nitty gritty! *The Oracle* is divided into seven chapters, each relating to a specific subject. Each subject also relates to one of the seven chakras. I talked about chakras in *girlosophy—A Soul Survival Kit* and *girlosophy²—The Love Survival Kit*. Briefly, the chakra system is an energy system based on the interrelationship of the energies of your mind, body, and spirit. The word "chakra" is Sanskrit, the ancient language of India, and it means "wheel of light." The chakra system is based on the concept that nothing occurs in the Universe that is not energetic and that as humans we're a complex system of energy centers: we are therefore all receivers and transmitters of energy. Any thought is simply another form of energy. To take this to the logical next step, we are microcosms of the Universe. Therefore the seven chakras within each of us are the gateways to the rest of the Universe—The Whole—and connect each of us to the other. On page 14 you'll find an overview of the chakra system.

There are two reasons for this structure and they each relate to how you can use *The Oracle* to best utilize the information you receive. First, by being divided into seven chapters by subject *The Oracle* gives you the maximum opportunity for increasing your understanding of yourself. It's for your personal growth! Secondly, the integration of each of these subjects with the chakra system gives you an additional opportunity to understand how a particular issue fits into and impacts upon other areas of your life. It's for your mind, body, and spirit. In other words, *The Oracle* is a truly holistic approach to connecting with the Universe.

HOW DO YOU USE *THE ORACLE*?

There are several ways you can use *The Oracle*, but it's entirely personal and there aren't any real rules as such. There's just a method or two to get you going and then after that it's over to you. One way or another the Universe will get the message to you, so feel free to be creative with the mode of request and delivery. It is meant to be flexible—just like you are!

The classic question is: "What is the likely outcome of ——?" (you fill in the situation or issue). This is useful for any general situation. However, I prefer the more active and specific question: "What is the best action or outcome I can take or accept right now for the highest good of all concerned?" This one's a beauty for when you have exhausted all other avenues!

AH, WHAT'S THE QUESTION AGAIN?

As in life, the better and more specific your question is, the more useful you'll find *The Oracle*'s response. Here are few questions to get you started.

To ask a question about the present: "What is my current situation?"

Or try: "What lesson do I need to learn at this time?"

To ask a question about the past: "What am I not releasing from the past?"

Or try: "What can I learn now to enable me to move on?"

To ask a question about the future: "What is the likely outcome of this situation?"

Or try: "How is my future affected by this situation?"

As you become more familiar with this book and more confident using it you will be better able to devise and tailor your own questions.

METHOD 1: **To use *The Oracle* in general**

If your question is not specific and you want to be guided by the Universe as to where you should be putting some heat or focus (energy!) then ask that question and open the book to any page. With this second method there's a bonus in that you'll be able to cross-refer to the specific chakra that your question relates to. Each chakra has its own properties. These properties give you additional ammunition to work with, because you can do some work directly on the relevant chakra to help you while you're getting things sorted.

METHOD 2: **To use *The Oracle* by chapter**

If you have a specific question that relates directly to a chapter (see the contents list for details), first find the relevant chapter, ask the question then flick to any page of that chapter for the message.

METHOD 3: **To use *The Oracle* by chakra**

A third method of using *The Oracle* involves tuning into the part of your body that relates to a particular chakra and selecting the matching chapter. For instance, if you feel tension in your solar plexus (below your rib cage) perhaps you are dealing with an emotional or willpower issue on which you may benefit from having some guidance, so you would then flip to the OMENS Chapter.

On page 14 there is a more detailed explanation of the chakra system and some tips for chakra-balancing. It's all to help you in your personal quest and to assist you to be a winner on this fun little obstacle course called Life!

METHOD 4: **To use *The Oracle* by the mandala**

The Oracle mandala is the colorful wheel at the front of the book. Around the edge are the seven chapters by subject. The mini mandalas in each "slice" relate to each chakra.

There are two ways to use the mandala:

1 Close your eyes and move your right finger onto the wheel. When you feel you are ready, move your right finger around the wheel and stop at whatever point you feel inclined. Wherever it lands, that's your chapter or chakra! Open it up and see what your message is!

2 If you need help or direction with a question, you can do step 1 and from the outcome you can ask a more specific question that relates to that chapter.

For example, if your finger lands on Truth—Throat chakra, questions you could ask might be: "What is the communication I need to deliver right now for the highest good of all concerned?" or "What is the truth of my current situation that I need to hear?"

AFFIRMATIONS: THINK IT, REPEAT IT, GET IT!

Making an affirmation is the final practical and important part of using *The Oracle*. Once you have read the entry you've chosen (or that the Universe has chosen for you!) a tremendously powerful thing to do is to make an affirmation based on the entry. Affirmations create the positive thought energy that is in alignment with the related chakra and maintaining its balance.

For example, say you open to the page in the Destiny Chapter, that reads "Hold out for the best." An appropriate affirmation might be: "I am worthy of the best in life and this is my personal destiny."

Affirmations should always be written or said in the present tense, as if they are already a part of your current experience. Spoken and written repetition of the affirmation helps to replace and reprogram negative thought energy. You can do it as many times as you wish. The greater the repetition and the more deliberate your intention to incorporate the affirmation the better the result. This is an important part of any personal growth program and I encourage you to make affirmations a regular part of your spiritual practice.

WHAT'S ON YOUR MIND?

Once you have asked a question and flipped to a page, for the message you receive to be effective it must resonate clearly and feel appropriate for you. As you read the message and absorb the full meaning it will translate into a form of knowledge or "knowingness"—what I call the "Aha!" factor.

The truth is, you have all the answers you need anyway. It's just sometimes, when there's a lot of static going on in your mind, it can be hard to pull out the answer you need! And that's the point: you'll only get the right answer (Aha!) if your mind is still and you're really focused before you open *The Oracle*.

Therefore, for maximum effectiveness a brief meditation session is recommended before you consult *The Oracle*. See page 12 for a quick step-by-step guide to meditation, or you can refer to *girlosophy—A Soul Survival Kit* (page 196) for a more general overview of the benefits of meditation and a brief introduction to some further techniques.

Sometimes *The Oracle*'s messages may seem deliberately and frustratingly oblique or obscure. It's up to you to draw your own conclusions from all that you see, hear or feel. You have to connect the dots in your own life in order to see your personal map. That's your responsibility: to find your way—with or without any overt assistance. So put on that detective cap and get cracking!

CHAPTER BY CHAKRA

The table of contents provides a list of areas covered by each chapter. As well, here's an overview of the chapters or chakras and what they mean for you.

SURVIVAL—BASE CHAKRA Your real life issues—the practical stuff. This is the chapter to go to if you're dealing with issues like whether you should move out of home, change your school or job or course or take out a loan! As the saying goes, fear is the opposite of faith and this is the chapter to consult if you need to be reminded of the benefits of keeping your faith.

KARMA—LOWER ABDOMEN CHAKRA This chapter is all about your actions! Look here if you want to see what you've sown or what you may reap. What's done may well be finished and in the past but remember that what goes around comes around. This chapter is all about your creative impulses and desires. So check it out.

OMENS—SOLAR PLEXUS OR POWER CHAKRA Listen carefully and watch for the signs! This is the chapter for hard-to-read situations where you need encouragement that you're reading the signs correctly. Underlying emotional issues and using your willpower are covered here.

LOVE—HEART CHAKRA What or who is in your heart? This chapter's in the middle so don't wear it out! Well, actually there's a good reason for it being in the middle: the heart is at the center of everything and love is the universal energy that connects all things. This chapter is all about love!

TRUTH—THROAT CHAKRA Speak up—go on, you know you want to! This is the chapter that gives you the good oil on what (or what not to) say. Communication is essential to your smooth journey in life and the more honest you are with yourself the easier it will be to be honest with others.

CROSSROADS—THIRD EYE CHAKRA It's time for a new path! Decisions, decisions … This chapter is for those major turning points in life that we all come to—the ones that can give you a headache! That's why this chapter is here: so there need be no more tears now.

DESTINY—CROWN CHAKRA Your true purpose awaits you: what are you waiting for? If you don't know what direction you should be going in life, this chapter can help! Plug into your universal mission and find out how your personal destiny will be revealed to you.

THE ORACLE TAKES YOU TO THE NEXT STEP!

By using *The Oracle* you can access the infinite intelligence of the Universe, and that's exactly what you're doing when you ask a higher power for help or for a message. That's where your chakras come into it too. Consciousness is the ultimate destination for all humans and that's what plugging into the Universe is all about—getting you reconnected, to keep you on the right path in life. Your chakras are the key to bringing you pure consciousness awareness. Tuning into energy—both within and around you—is the way to manifest your true purpose in life. *The Oracle* will help to tune you into the right frequency so you're right on point.

And remember, the essential element of any exercise is to have fun, so enjoy the process and don't take things too seriously.

As always, I wish you the best
of everything on your journey …

Anthea Paul [2002]

Meditation

To make an effective request of the Universe your mind needs to be static-free—free, that is, from too many overlapping and conflicting thoughts. When you desire a clear response you have to make a clear request, in the same way as when you're talking to someone. Thoughts are energy. So if you send a thought out among a bunch of other jumbled-up thoughts it has a greater chance of getting lost in the maelstrom.

If you find that having asked your question you flick to a page in the book and don't get some sort of an "Aha!" feeling when you read the answer, it's likely you were in the static zone!

Meditation helps you clear the static. It's a heightened form of concentration that can be a very calming and powerful method of rewiring yourself for positivity and enhanced focus on any goal.

There are many methods of meditation and (as with anything) only you can decide which method works best for you. To get you started, here's a brief rundown on a meditation technique that may help you become clear, focused and static-free! If after a reasonable number of attempts this method doesn't seem to be effective for you, research or experiment with other techniques.

The method described below is the breath observation method, and it should get you into the zone if you practice it. Choose a time when you won't be disturbed by anyone. This is your precious time.

Preparation: First, take off your watch and put it close by so you can check the time. You may even prefer to set an alarm clock for a few minutes' time. Get comfortable by either sitting on your bed with your feet on the floor or sitting on the floor with your legs crossed and your spine against a wall for support. You can even sit on a chair or lie on the floor. Whatever feels right for you.

Step 1. Breathe in through your nose with your mouth closed.

Step 2. Leave your eyes either half-open and focused on one point in the room or, if you prefer, close them fully.

Step 3. Continue to breathe through your nose until you feel the breath go all the way to your stomach, and then breathe out the same way so you can feel a kind of "loop" pattern in your breathing.

Step 4. Don't follow any train of thought (I know this is hard but you have to try). If any thoughts arise, let them fall away as you return your focus to your breath.

Step 5. The thoughts will continue to come—the trick is to learn to ignore them. They have no place for you right now because they are only serving to distract you from your mission of being peacefully static-free! If you find you have too many thoughts, practice saying an affirmation over and over in your mind: for example, "I love my life. I am happy and contented. All is well in my world." You can change the affirmation to suit your needs or your mood.

Step 6. Be still, don't fidget and really try to control any excess body movement. Focus.

Step 7. Do this for as long as you can. You can start with a few minutes and work up to longer periods. Do it first thing in the morning when you're fresh, and then again in the evening before you go to sleep.

The more you meditate, the greater the results—but you'll have to do a bit of work!

The Chakra

YOUR ENERGY HOTSPOTS!

As a girlosopher you're aware that you have a physical life, a mental life and a spiritual life. And as you know, you exist on all of these material, psychological and spiritual planes at the same time. The connections between these dimensions are your chakras—what I call energy hotspots that are located in your body—which are also the connections between you and the universal energy flow. Combined they form a system which governs your experience on the earthly and spiritual planes.

WHAT'S THE POINT OF THE CHAKRA SYSTEM?

Your chakras are the keys to healing any dis-ease existing between your mind, body, and spirit. You can feel when things are not quite flowing in your life (or worse!) and normally this will be associated with an illness in the region of the chakra you need to work on. As you can see it's pretty crucial to understand and get in touch with your chakras because they can really help you on your journey towards wholeness—and as a girlosopher!

WHAT DOES "CHAKRA" MEAN?

"Chakra" is Sanskrit, the old Indian language still used in certain literary circles, and it's from the Hindu religion and philosophy. Chakra means "wheel of light." We all originally came from light and these wheels are our connections to the the Universe, the ultimate light source.

The philosopher and psychologist Carl Jung referred to the chakras as "gateways to consciousness." He believed that through these gateways a person could communicate with the Universe and receive cosmic energies in return. All of which may sound pretty far out but the proof is in the being! Jung's view is consistent with the Hindu system. The chakras are sometimes also referred to and symbolized by lotuses, the revered flower of the East. The lotus, with its roots in the mud and its petals open to the sky, is representative of the process of enlightenment.

HOW DO CHAKRAS WORK?

Chakras are the energy centers in your "auric" body that are linked to your physical body. It's as if you have a cosmic form of your own physical body that is pure energy and, invisible though it may be, it emanates and resonates with every thought, action and reaction that you have—it's always with you. Another way to think about it is scientifically: we are matter and as all matter is energy (according to Newton's theory) therefore we are just another form of energy.

WHAT'S YOUR VIBE?

As an individual ball of energy you "vibrate" at different levels. Your thoughts are forms of energy that have an impact on your cosmic body as well as your physical body, which in turn affects your "vibe."

System

Some people emit good vibes while others don't! You need to think positive thoughts to change the energy you project. So now you know why it's all about the positive (and good) vibrations.

YOU GO, COSMIC GIRL!

The chakras are the focal energy points vibrating at a particular frequency. Each chakra has a related color to which it resonates and each chakra in turn is connected to particular organs in the body. In addition, the chakras are connected to correlating energy bands on your aura. If this is hard to get your head around, think of it as the energy that's given off by your body, the way food gives off an aroma while it's being cooked. Like wheels the chakras "spin" in constant rotation, reflecting an energy from the body that is constantly in effect. Cosmic? You bet you are!

WHERE DO I FIND EACH OF THE CHAKRAS?

Traditionally, there are seven chakras. Each chakra is associated with a particular region of the body, each has a purpose and each is a source for healing therapy. Here's a quick list:

1 Base chakra (located directly underneath the base of your pelvis)

2 Lower abdomen chakra, also known as the sex chakra (just below your navel)

3 Solar plexus or power chakra (located under your rib cage)

4 Heart chakra (center of your chest)

5 Throat chakra (center and front of your neck region)

6 Third eye chakra (between your eyebrows)

7 Crown chakra (top of the head in the center).

ARE YOUR CHAKRAS IN BALANCE OR OUT OF WHACK?

When any of the chakras are out of balance, healing is required. You can tell when your chakras are in balance. Everything feels good, you feel on track and on purpose and you have a clear view of your unique role in life. When your chakras are balanced you're in tune with the Universal flow or vibe.

Rebalancing the chakras restores vitality to your body as well as unity to their combined functioning. Mantras (repeated affirmations or prayers while you meditate) and tones (for example, the word "om" hummed at a certain level) rebalance each chakra. Massage is another way.

Ultimately, having and maintaining one's chakras in balance is essential for your individual soul to be united with the collective or universal soul. It's an intuitive thing, too: often we know instinctively what's causing our physical problems but we lack the necessary knowledge or the courage to work on the source directly. Think of it this way: if you put one vertebra in your back out, it affects your whole back. The chakras function in exactly the same way.

Below is a breakdown of the chakras' properties and qualities. These can be used to show you what kind of question you may need to ask *The Oracle* and therefore which section will be the most useful for you to refer to.

FIRST CHAKRA: BASE CHAKRA
Where do you find it? Base of the spine, under the pelvis.

What's it all about? You, as an individual, are linked with the world in a physical form. The base chakra is the foundation of existence upon which the personality is built, in ultimate connection to the Divine Source. Here your self-expression and ambition are tempered by the desire to evolve and protect yourself. Basically it's all about survival!

What's your mantra? I am understood and I express myself as a physical being, and I am constantly evolving.

Related body parts Adrenal glands, lymph system, colon and intestines, bones, teeth, nails, legs, arms.

Associated color Red.

In balance? You recognize the material world is the ground level of existence but you maintain a clear view to the spiritual. In this state you are still deeply connected to nature and yet you trust implicitly in universal laws. You seek stability, and self-reliance and independence are your end goals. You have appropriate personal boundaries in place and you respect the boundaries of others. Good one!

Out of whack? The material world is overwhelmingly your focus, and you disregard and ignore matters of spiritual concern. The pursuit of personal material gain is your sole purpose and your ego rules your basic survival instinct, preventing your heart from alerting you to universal energies. Insecurity, greed and stress are your primary life experiences. You have an inability to let go and to "flow and let flow." Your personal boundaries are weak and you crash in on the boundaries of others without consideration. Phew!

SECOND CHAKRA: LOWER ABDOMEN CHAKRA
Where do you find it? Lower abdomen to the navel area.

What's it all about? This chakra is the center of creativity, relationships, and sexuality. The "male" and "female" energies are harmoniously blended and balanced to create relationships, which serve the intentions of the Divine Source.

What's your mantra? I express and give birth to my Self by using the sex drive to channel creativity and beauty.

Related body parts Genitals, reproductive organs, spleen, bladder, kidneys.

Associated color Orange.

In balance? You give and receive in equal measure without difficulty. You're a star! You surrender to the process of sharing and your relationships are harmonious and deeply connected. Your openness of heart, body and mind ensure that joy is your life experience. Your sexuality is expressed with unity and spiritual transcending.

Out of whack? You have an inability to give or receive and find it hard to surrender to universal energies. You may be locked into the purely physical or functional expression of sexuality. You try to control situations and emotions in relationships, which leads to needs and (healthy) expression being repressed. Jealousy and mistrust are symptoms of a closed heart, mind, and body.

THIRD CHAKRA: SOLAR PLEXUS OR POWER CHAKRA

Where do you find it? The solar plexus (under the rib cage) including the region above the navel.

What's it all about? This chakra rules the impulses and is the center of desire. Your personality is integrated here with your impulses, your free will, wishes and the expression of personal power. That's why it's often referred to as the power chakra!

What's your mantra? I am a being who expresses my personality through my free will and in accordance with my desires.

Related body parts Adrenal glands, pancreas, nervous system, abdomen, lower back, stomach, liver, spleen, digestive system, gall bladder.

Associated color Yellow.

In balance? Your emotions are vital and free-flowing! You have an overriding sense of tranquility and you generally exist in a state of calmness. Free will and personal power are each exercised intuitively and spontaneously without fear. Basically, you're pretty cool.

Out of whack? Well, it goes like this: emotional blockages are common and panic is the overwhelming feeling. You are incapable of trusting in the process or "going with the flow" and you place too much emphasis on getting your own way, ignoring the better solution for the greater good. Anger, fear, and hatred are common responses.

FOURTH CHAKRA: HEART CHAKRA

Where do you find it? Center of chest, heart region.

What's it all about? Your heart is the heart of the chakra system! It is the mediator between the top three and the lower three chakras. It is the great processor through which all emotion, compassion and intuition is channeled. It's doing a lot of work if you're in sync! Healing and emotions are generated and balanced by free-flowing love.

What's your mantra? I love my Self and this love is expressed to the whole, which is equally loved.

Related body parts Heart, circulatory or arterial system, rib cage, upper back, arms, lungs, hands.

Associated color Green.

In balance? Unconditional love is freely offered and your connection to the spiritual and the physical world (the natural environment) reflects your state of passion, bliss and joy. You tend to see and accept the positive aspects in all events in life. To you, no matter what, it's ALL good!

Out of whack? Problems with the heart recur. Anger and fear rule your reactions and impulses. Freedom from worry is all but impossible. You may not have the ability to be compassionate and selfishness becomes habitual. Love given is conditional and transactional in nature. Ka-ching!

FIFTH CHAKRA: THROAT CHAKRA

Where do you find it? The throat area, underneath the chin and above the inner collarbone.

What's it all about? This chakra relates to how you communicate your emotions. It also assists you in the transition towards inward reflection. It's the base for all aspects of sound on the physical and vibrational (or metaphysical) planes. It's your voice, your laughter, how you cry, shout or whisper. It's your Self as you truly express it!

What's your mantra? I am a being who is freely able to communicate my essence to the Universe.

Related body parts Throat, thyroid, vocal cords, lungs, neck.

Associated colors Cyan, turquoise, light blue.

In balance? Harmonious, powerful and clear communication of the truth. You face and express reality easily and readily without fear or favor. It's ON! You are creatively tuned into the divine, and you are powerful as a communicator, even when you are silent. You trust and act upon your intuition above all and without hesitation.

Out of whack? Your knowledge is not communicated well or wisely. Um, er, things are misinterpreted or misunderstood and your explanations are clouded or distorted perceptions of the truth. Hmmm … Ignorance or a lack of discernment can be a symptom of imbalance in this chakra as well as mild to chronic depression. You have a fear of speaking your truth. Oops.

SIXTH CHAKRA: THIRD EYE CHAKRA

Where do you find it? Center of the forehead between the eyes or eyebrows.

What's it all about? You perceive yourself as actually "being." Your psychic qualities (including your sixth sense!) are activated and your awareness brings you a sense of the cosmic. Concentration and focus leads to the growth of your intuition, your basic instinct! You understand the spiritual connection that is truly who you are. This chakra is described as being the gateway for spiritual understanding. It's deep!

What's your mantra? I am a "knowing" being for whom awareness is all.

Related body parts Pituitary gland, left eye, sinus, nose, ears.

Associated colors Indigo, deep marine blue.

In balance? Your psychic, clairvoyant, and intuitive side is very active! Vivid dreams are common when your third eye chakra is in balance. Great wisdom and creative solutions are easy to attain (well, they seem easier anyway!). The signs on your spiritual path become easier to read as your awareness level increases.

Out of whack? You only think about the material things in life—spiritual matters don't concern you. It's all about you and your needs. Your intellect dominates your activities and yet concentration is difficult. Your conscious mind is often overwhelmed by too many fearful, negative, and conflicting thoughts. Spooky stuff!

SEVENTH CHAKRA: CROWN CHAKRA

Where do you find it? At the top of your head, in the center.

What's it all about? This chakra is where you (as a beautiful and unique individual!) and the Universe actually connect. The crown chakra represents the culmination of the other six chakras, for here the complete physical, mental and spiritual human is connected with its higher Self and the Source: pure consciousness.

What's your mantra? I am a pure being with no limitations.

Related body parts Central nervous system, pineal gland, right eye, brain, cerebellum, skull.

Associated colors Violet, white, gold.

In balance? You see yourself as being connected to the Divine Source and as a unique individual who is part of the whole. You focus on the greater good and "consciousness," not just on what your own needs are. You're a giver in the fullest sense and you do it not for personal gain but because you love to and it brings joy to all concerned.

Out of whack? Oh dear! Lets see now: egocentricity, recurring fears, worries, a sense of confusion, depression, you may lack inspiration and/or just have a general sense of dissatisfaction with life. Hmmm. It's quite a list!

IT'S ALL ABOUT ENERGY!

So, from the fairly exhaustive list above you should be able to see (and feel) where you're at. Figuring out your energy levels in each chakra may not be easy at first but once you become really familiar with the properties and classic symptoms of each you'll soon be able to do it without checking, which is the aim of the whole exercise.

The more you can tune into yourself in order to self-diagnose and heal the better your questions will be and the more accurate your messages from *The Oracle* will be. Soon you'll be able to cope and deal with whatever gets thrown your way!

LIFE ISSUES

PRACTICAL STUFF

FEAR VERSUS FAITH

PHYSICALITY

INSTINCT

DOING VERSUS BEING

AMBITION

FORMATION OF SELF

SURVIVAL

PERSONALITY

PROTECTION OF SELF

SUCCESS VERSUS FAILURE

SURVIVAL

[base chakra]

All your actions are either a movement away from order or a movement towards it. What's your intention?

You can't figure everything out all at once. Life is a fact-finding mission! You need to hunt and gather information and prioritize it. Then you can methodically work your way down the list.

Sometimes a new entry affects something you thought you had dealt with already. Whatever this new piece of the puzzle is, it has come up for a good reason: to force you to re-examine your priorities. Life's an ongoing task of re-assessment based on the latest news to hand. Deal with it to the best of your abilities. Because that's the whole point of the exercise.

go

GO GENTLY.

GO DIRECTLY.

GO INTENTIONALLY.

GO AHEAD.

GO GET 'EM!

YOU'RE GOING WELL.

JUST KEEP GOING!

HONOR YOURSELF. LOOK AFTER YOURSELF. NOW MORE THAN EVER.

It's pretty simple, really.

MAXIMIZE
YOUR EXISTING
RESOURCES.
GET MORE OUT
OF LESS.

Whether you're training your mind to be still or training your body to perform a particular function or skill, it's a long process. The key is to maintain passion and commitment over time—stay fresh, stay the distance. With time you'll achieve the ultimate breakthroughs that focused endeavor brings.

Then push yourself beyond any limits you gave yourself. This will give you self-confidence and the desire to go even further. Push a bit harder and see what gives. Then do it again.

Whatever happened to you in the past was for your spiritual evolution. Now, to say "It's for your own good, dear," may be irritating (sorry!), but you need to believe that everything that happens always has an upside. It's a big ask, but you have to overcome all feelings of disappointment and bitterness that things didn't necessarily go in your favor. This may take some time, but you need to believe that you will never feel the same way again. Your feelings about each situation will therefore be unique. Have courage! Try not to become cynical or permanently disillusioned. When you remain positive you'll see that things pan out for you beautifully.

Love

THROUGH LOVING ACCEPTANCE OF
YOURSELF YOU CAN TRULY FACE YOUR FEARS
AND YOUR PAIN AND

yourself

TRANSFORM THEM INTO STRENGTH,
UNDERSTANDING, AND COMPASSION.

first

Personal boundaries are critical. Set them in place and you will undoubtedly get reactions—positive and negative—from others. Perhaps no one will want to acknowledge your right to set your personal boundaries in any way that suits you. Instead you may be accused of being heartless, selfish or egocentric. But in fact it's in everyone's interest that you do, no matter what your perceived or actual motivation is. By setting your own limits, others can learn from you. They'll learn from not getting things their own way all the time. They may see you in a different light too. This is a profound lesson for each of you.

limits

Building a solid structure—of your career, your lifestyle, friendships or relationships, requires commitment. To make it last you need to devote a certain amount of energy to the task. Only you can decide how much energy is required. And only you can follow through to completion. But if the foundation hasn't been laid properly the whole structure will be shaky. Commitment is the foundation of any achievement.

fear

FEAR AND FAITH ARE ETERNALLY MARRIED
TO EACH OTHER. YOU NEED MASSES OF FAITH
TO OVERCOME MASSES OF FEAR.

faith

To change yourself you need to take a risk. If you're always concerned about protecting yourself you may never take the risk that will ultimately set you free. You can never be protected from yourself, in any case.

Take responsibility for your own trip. Carry your own bags, pay your own way and write your own itinerary. Back yourself at every turn and you will have the fulfillment of knowing that you're the safety zone you've always longed for.

GET AROUND IT.
IF YOU CAN'T GET
OVER IT, THAT IS.

Because you're a work in progress; be gentle with yourself when you have to face a situation you've never come across before. You may be in transition or in a difficult phase, which means you're learning to cope with a new set of circumstances. Just do the best you can with the variables you've been given. You're off the hook!

goals

Setting goals for yourself is smart, challenging, and fun. Being nakedly ambitious is not the same thing. Tread lightly when you're expressing your desires to achieve something. Remember that the people who achieve their stated goals or ambitions are usually those who recognize how others have contributed to their success. Be cool. Push quietly and effectively—you don't need to be a bulldozer to get where you want to go.

Sometimes chocolate is the only thing that works.

If you sometimes
feel you need more
support than you're
getting, remember
that you are always
supported by the
Universe. You're
never truly alone.
Your vulnerability
will then be your
strength and you'll
find new ways of
doing things.

Your body requires your attention. You may need to give it an overhaul so it can not only survive but thrive. Perhaps you should embark on a detoxification program or a new vitamin regime or perhaps you simply need to drink more water. The Universe now points you in the right direction for the right treatment. Tune into what your body wants—and look out for that spa offer!

personality

Your personality is developing in ways that surprise those around you. You're not predictable at the moment, which is new to people, even those closest to you who think they know you well. This is your chance to try on a few different hats. After all, you never agreed to wear just one! Enjoy this new-found freedom to express yourself. You're having fun and by honoring yourself you are poised for all sorts of interesting encounters.

SPIRIT

UNDAUNTED

REALITY

VOW

INNER STRENGTH

VICTORY

AFFIRMATION

LOVE

IT'S ALL ABOUT SURVIVAL.

survival

Is it just your ego talking?

Can you step outside your own internal–external dialogue for a moment and see your life from a higher perspective? What's in it for you (and your ego) if you don't? The Universe wants you to answer some (hard) questions!

Your instincts are sharp and you are riding high on the discipline that comes with picking your way carefully and methodically through the maze. You are sure-footed and you have no fear. Your end goal is the reward of controlling nothing and yet being controlled by nothing. You are in the perfect zone of acceptance and intuition. This is MASTERY.

The job or position you seek is the one you will come to re-evaluate further down the track. Everything that currently attracts you to it will become the very things that test and finally repel you. Knowing this you can be on the lookout for the change in the energy. The Universe wants us to experience duality (yin and yang) in all things. Then it's your move—again!

Always try to keep one eye on the horizon—never turn your back on your future. When you see a wave coming you have two choices: swim towards it consciously, deliberately, and with respect or get out of the way fast!

Sea change

RE-EVALUATE
what you call your
failures. They can only be
assessed in the context of your
successes. Did you fail to act or
did your so-called failure to act
save you in that situation? Only
you know the context. And
it's all a question of
context.

FIND THE COMMON GROUND.

ENERGY IN + COMMON GOALS

= ENERGY OUT + SUCCESS

ENERGY

WORLD

COMPANY

BOY/GIRL

FAMILY

EDUCATION

OUTPUT

COMMON

GOALS

INPUT

COUNTRY

EMPLOYEE

GIRL/BOY

CAREER

STUDENT

Your network is your support system. This interaction with others leads to interdependence

NETWORK = SUPPORT

INTERACTION = INTERDEPENDENCE

which leads to growth. Sharing is essential to the survival of us all.

SHARING = SURVIVAL

49

Be clear on what your basic needs are. The survival mechanism is there to serve you. It is both the badge of progress and the underpinning structure necessary to develop the Self. It reflects the greater, ultimate journey: the journey of the soul.

Life is not about snatching the largest piece of the pie for yourself. There's plenty to go around. Always. The Universe is infinitely abundant, so start thinking in those terms. What can you do to expand the possibilities and the potential of the task you have in front of you?

ACTIONS

REACTIONS

CREATIVE IMPULSES

SEXUALITY

RELATIONSHIPS

BEAUTY

PHYSICALITY VERSUS SPIRITUALITY

EXPRESSION OF NEEDS

EXPRESSION OF DESIRES

52

KARMA

[lower abdomen chakra]

Water finds its own level

If someone says they're not good enough for you, believe them. By saying this they're letting you know they don't feel good enough about themselves to meet you as an equal. And if they don't feel they have mastery over their life they probably have low self-esteem. Until their self-esteem improves it will be difficult for them to love you unconditionally.

"A lot of people say you need drive to realize your talent, but the truth is, your talent is your drive."

[Stevie Wonder]

Choice is power. You can choose
to act, react, change, and adapt.
And any time you choose you can
choose to re-invent yourself. All
it takes is time, willpower, and
self-discipline. Re-invention is a
powerful choice. It's the active,
creative, and dynamic process of
owning your desires and acting in
accordance with their ebb and flow.
When you act on your desires you
are truly free. Free to make choices.
Free to change. And free to be.

Listen to the voice inside your head. It's not idle chatter. Your inner voice whispers your dreams and lists the temptations on offer, dangling promises of a better life before you. It's the real voice of reason and it's daring you to make a power move! Honor it by deciding whatever it is that you want in life: right here and right now.

Something new
is transforming
your ability to
manifest what
you now want
in your
relationships.
You are
honoring your-
self and using
your gifts. You
can only
generate what
you believe is
possible, and
you now have a
vision for the
future that will
bring you all the
things you
desire.

beauty

THE ULTIMATE BEAUTY IS YOUR INNER BEAUTY.
YOU ARE BEING CHALLENGED TO RECOGNIZE
YOUR BEAUTY ABOVE ALL. ONCE YOU CAN SEE
YOUR TRUE LIGHT, THE UNIVERSE WILL REWARD
YOU BY BRINGING MORE BEAUTY INTO YOUR LIFE
THAN YOU DREAMED COULD BE POSSIBLE.

YOU ARE PRESENTLY CAUGHT BETWEEN THE PHYSICAL NATURE OF YOUR BEING AND THE BURGEONING SPIRITUAL EXPRESSION OF YOURSELF THAT IS TRYING TO EMERGE. IF YOU BLOCK YOUR INTUITION YOU MAY BE IGNORING SOMETHING CRITICAL. WHAT IS THE POINT OF HOLDING YOURSELF BACK? YOU NEED TO ALLOW YOUR SPIRITUAL SIDE TO DEVELOP IN ORDER TO BALANCE YOUR DOMINANT MATERIAL EXISTENCE. THIS IS JUST A TEST BUT YOU ARE BEING ASKED TO STEP UP!

IT'S OKAY! YOUR CURRENT ACTIONS ARE IN LINE WITH YOUR DESTINY.

YOUR SEXUALITY IS THE SOURCE OF YOUR TRUE CREATIVITY. WHAT CREATIVE PROJECTS HAVE BEEN BURNING A HOLE IN YOUR DESKTOP? WHAT IDEA ARE YOU AFRAID OF EXPLORING? GO WITH THE URGE AND MAKE IT HAPPEN. TAKE A RISK FOR GOODNESS' SAKE! NOW IS THE TIME TO EXPERIMENT.

LEAVE THINGS AS THEY ARE. EVERYTHING IS ABSOLUTELY AS IT SHOULD BE. IT'S ALL PERFECT.

The union you have been seeking is almost within your grasp. The right partner appears for you at the right time. When you're ready for the final hurdle—letting go of your set notions of what this person is like—an opportunity for a real and profound partnership will reveal itself.

Identify the real source of your hunger and rename it desire. How does this desire look? It may be either intellectual, sexual, emotional, psychological or spiritual, or a combination of some or all of these. Once you have identified the type of desire you're experiencing you can act upon it and harness your energies to create whatever it is you truly want.

desire

Inspire
and be inspired!

How can you listen to your whispering heart if you're constantly rushing about in traffic, in your head ... in life? Allow yourself the time to breathe. Being still generates creativity, which only appears when you're in flow or in sync. Being creative doesn't just mean doodling on a sketch pad or tinkering on the piano (although both of these help!). Designing your life is a creative exercise which requires careful consideration—on an ongoing basis. And creativity makes for better decision making.

So take a deep breath ....

BE ACTIVE NOT PASSIVE

BE ASSERTIVE NOT
AGGRESSIVE

BE FREE AND NOT RESTRICTED

THESE ARE THE KEY ASPECTS
INDICATED FOR YOUR HIGHEST
EVOLUTION RIGHT NOW

Each time you stake a claim on your future by asking clearly for

something you want you're asking for something far different in

reality. What you're really asking for is the opportunity to become

who you truly are and who you can become. This is the real ASK.

And you can bet you will receive.

YOUR JOURNEY IS WHAT'S IMPORTANT AND THE DESIRES YOU EXPERIENCE WHILE ON THE PATH ARE SIMPLY FUEL FOR YOUR FUTURE. DON'T DENY THEM—YOUR DESIRES NEED TO GET A LIFE! IN ORDER TO FULLY EXPRESS THEM YOU MUST EXPLORE AND FOLLOW THEM, THEN REAP THE REWARD OF THE SOUL: PERSONAL GROWTH.

The generosity you show yourself will soon be manifested in the generosity others show you. Start with yourself—show kindness, compassion, and love—and this internal shift will see a parallel shift in the external world.

Loving another person is hard. But loving yourself is perhaps the most difficult task you'll face. You can't truly love another until you love yourself, because loving someone else means accepting, honoring, and loving their destiny as you do your own. Remember, at certain points your path may merge with or verge from theirs. Acceptance is essential. Love it all.

Respect the type of energy you pull in: good or bad, it's what you have manifested by your thoughts. If you take responsibility for everything in your life, you'll see only true beauty all around you.

A BLANK PAGE OR CANVAS IS A CHALLENGE FOR AN ARTIST. AS AN ARTIST OF LIFE YOUR CHALLENGE COMES THROUGH NEW BEGINNINGS. WHETHER IT'S A NEW RELATIONSHIP, JOB, HOME OR LIFESTYLE, ASK YOURSELF, "HOW DO I EXPRESS MYSELF IN THIS NEW STAGE?" HOWEVER IT TURNS OUT IS HOWEVER YOUR IMAGINATION WANTS IT TO.

You can never assume to know the temperature of a relationship. A relationship is dynamic and changes monthly, daily or sometimes hourly! You have to reassess it again and again on an ongoing basis. You need to be in tune so you'll know if there are any pressure systems brewing. If you're experiencing apprehension in dealing with your relationships, they may be in a weather-checking phase. Just go easy. You'll be all right if you do.

Your current actions set you up for all future reactions. Sometimes you may sow a seed (for better or worse) without realizing. So consider your recent thoughts and how you acted as a result. What thoughts do you need to have and what actions do you need to take now to generate the results you truly deserve?

How are you going?

Carefully mark your progress by taking stock along the path. Is it smooth or bumpy? Are you traveling quickly or slowly? Are you flowing with things or have you been in stop–start mode? Are you a bit lost (go on, admit it) or do you know exactly how and where you're going? An assessment is vital if you're to stay on your chosen path. So don't put it off! Otherwise, you may end up somewhere that looks nothing like the place you expected. And then you've got the added hassle of trying to get back.

FIRST YOU'VE GOT TO GET OVER IT. THEN YOU'VE GOT TO GET OVER THEM.

Regard all dealings with people as relationships, not just encounters. Then you'll see that each person has equal weight. You'll be much more effective in any negotiations or dealings once you are both on the level.

REINVENTION IS YOUR PASSPORT
TO YOUR (MORE GLORIOUS)
FUTURE. REINVENTION IS
RENEWAL OF MIND, BODY, SPIRIT.
REINVENTION IS THE ONLY WAY
TO SURVIVE.

reinvention

If you want
your private life
to stay private, you'll
have to keep it
that way

Commitment is active, not passive. Commitment is doing whatever you can to bring about the desired result. Anything less is half-hearted.

OMENS

SIGNS

FREE WILL

PERSONAL POWER

EMOTIONS

DESIRE

INTUITION

FLOW

HARMONY

TRUST

OMENS

[solar plexus or power chakra]

84

If someone is acting strangely around you, such as ignoring you or avoiding you, and you honestly know that you've done nothing to them, take a closer look at the dynamics. The chances are they believe they have in some way exposed themselves to you and they are projecting their shame or embarrassment onto you. Take the time to make them feel comfortable about whatever it is they (think) they have done and maybe you'll each go to a new level of understanding together.

The source of everything you need flows directly from your heart.

Flow and let flow

conflicting emotions are understandable

in the face of certain change. Sorting those emotions out, however,

could prove more difficult than undertaking change. Emotionally

you may feel as though you're on a tightrope. Try to walk lightly.

Trusting yourself is one of the first steps on the spiritual path. Once you trust yourself you can consolidate your beliefs and agenda. With the knowledge and security that you'll always be able to find a way around problems or situations that crop up from time to time you'll see the positive results of vesting faith in yourself. And that in turn propels you onwards.

WHAT'S YOUR (REAL) INTENTION?

free will

Choice is often the precursor of fear and always the initiator of free will. Act to exercise your free will. Direct your outward actions towards choices that will serve your destiny. As the saying goes, "Check yourself before you wreck yourself!" Fear must be controlled or transmuted if you want personal growth, but fear can be useful to show you exactly where you may need to go. Fear is not the only option: choice is.

YOU WILL BE AT PEACE EMOTIONALLY

THE VERY INSTANT YOU DECIDE TO BE.

WITH AWARENESS AND A HEALTHY

DOSE OF DETACHMENT YOU CAN

EXERCISE YOUR RIGHT TO CHOOSE

WHICH EMOTION SERVES YOU MOMENT

TO MOMENT. NOW THAT'S A NEW

FEELING!

The flower you pick today will have only a short life. But for the moment it is beautiful and appears perfect. Its perfection is an illusion, however, because already it is changing. Once the petals reveal the change it's too late to save it. Enjoy it while it lasts.

Practice is the cornerstone of any achievement, small or large. One task practiced with dedication becomes the platform for the next. And so on. Until you've climbed Mount Everest.

It only takes one line, one phone call, one (chance) meeting or one supposed "coincidence" to alert you to a new course of action you could take in your life. A coincidence indicates that your destiny is trying to make itself known to you. Look out. All the signs are there that you're about to go in a whole new direction.

KEEP YOUR EYES ON THE PRIZE!

Deal with what you've
actually been given.
Don't expend precious
energy pursuing things
you think you should
have received. If you
focus on the gaps
you'll end up with more
of the same. Life is
about maximizing the
advantages in front
of you. The hand you
were dealt is the
one you're meant to
play with.

YOU HAVE THE TRUMP CARDS.
BUT IT'S UP TO YOU TO DECIDE HOW
TO PLAY THEM.

IF YOU'RE GETTING TOO MUCH RESISTANCE, IT'S A (BIG) SIGN THAT THERE'S ANOTHER WAY. BLOCKAGES AND DEAD ENDS ARE THERE TO SERVE YOU, TO SHOW WHEN YOU NEED TO TAKE THE HARD DECISIONS OR TO CHANGE YOUR APPROACH. RESISTANCE CAN HELP YOU, BECAUSE BY RECOGNIZING IT FOR WHAT IT REALLY IS—AN ALLY ON YOUR JOURNEY—YOU WILL REACH YOUR DESTINY POINT SOONER.

Whatever you're doing—leaving a relationship, moving house, changing jobs, saving money—set yourself a deadline. If there's something you know you're putting off or you're not committing to, check your diary and pin yourself to a date. This will be a commitment you will have made to yourself. Only when you actually commit to yourself does the Universe reward you. Commitment is its own end. You'd better step up!

SELF-KNOWLEDGE
WILL PROPEL
YOU FORWARD.
SELF-DENIAL
IS A PART OF
YOUR PAST. AND
IT NO LONGER
SERVES YOU.

It's not all about you, even if you've been told that it is! And what you don't receive in life can often define you more than what you're given.

You may need to be rejected, denied, overlooked, bypassed or ignored to be reminded of the nature of humility. Don't freak out or become overly sensitive. It's no big deal and it happens to everyone all the time. Understand this and you'll understand that there will be a next time!

Humility can shape you and make you stronger. Used properly it can strengthen your resolve to get something. Being humbled can sharpen your appetite for success. Make it work for you!

humility

Your unrealistic
expectations are
setting you up for
a disappointment.

How can you
overcome this?
By understanding
that your happiness
does not depend
on the outcome of
any one event or
relationship.

Be open to all
possibilities

Stay cool.

The time calls for emotional discipline. When those around you are getting carried away your restraint is essential as a counterbalance. Letting your emotions run riot may make things worse than they actually are. Try and keep things in perspective.

Your complete trust in the Universe is well placed. However, you must take a practical approach to complement your faith that things are going to work out well. It's no good playing hooky and hiding from your responsibilities, hoping the Universe will make things easy for you regardless. It won't necessarily, because the Universe is also a taskmaster that wants to see you dedicate yourself to your purpose. If you're naughty you'll pay a price of some sort!

Trust is non-negotiable.
It's either there or it's not.

103

Your confidence will give you the endurance you'll need for this part of the journey. Nothing may seem easy on this stretch of the marathon, but self-assurance makes up for a whole lot. You know you can do it. So stick at it.

Whatever you see, hear, and experience in the world around you is a reflection of yourself. How you experience the world is a constant monitor of how you've been thinking about yourself and others. Knowing this, you can never blame anyone else for what happens in your life. It's called taking responsibility. Do it and you will truly be on your way to your spiritual evolution.

105

left field

Coming—ready or not!

Something may happen on your path that seems unbelievable. It may have come up so unexpectedly you feel as though it's straight out of left field. And you're not sure you're ready for it! Unexpected though it may be, you have created this opportunity. You just need to adjust to the fact that it's here whether you're ready for it or not.

YOU ARE A POWERFUL BEING. TAKE RESPONSIBILITY FOR YOUR CREATIONS.

signs

IF YOU HAVE BEEN
PRESENTED WITH NEW
CLUES REGARDING HOW TO
MAKE THINGS HAPPEN,
IGNORE THEM TO YOUR
DETRIMENT. WHAT WAS
PREVIOUSLY A REMOTE
POSSIBILITY IS NOW A
VIABLE PROBABILITY. ACT
IN ACCORDANCE WITH THE
SIGNS YOU HAVE BEEN
SHOWN.

When you feel overwhelmed emotionally give yourself an instant break and take time out till you settle down. You can't always be expected to cope like a robot, and automated responses are not what's called for now.

LOVE

HEART

INTUITION

MEDIATION

COMPASSION

PROCESS

UNCONDITIONALITY

PASSION

BLISS

FREEDOM

LOVE

[heart chakra]

On the other side of fear is freedom. Only when you feel that you are truly free can you be creative, happy and fulfilled in life. The process of understanding your own heart is the process of moving through fear into the freedom of unconditional love and happiness.

" Through money or power you cannot solve all problems. The problem in the human heart must first be solved. "

His Holiness, The Dalai Lama

NO MATTER WHAT THE ISSUE IS, LOVE IS THE CORRECT RESPONSE.

Compassion is the greatest skill you can develop in life. Compassion allows you to overcome all obstacles and to share in the triumphs and sorrows of others. Even when it seems as though you were not on the winning team, you can be by being compassionate. When properly experienced, compassion allows you to be a winner all the time.

116

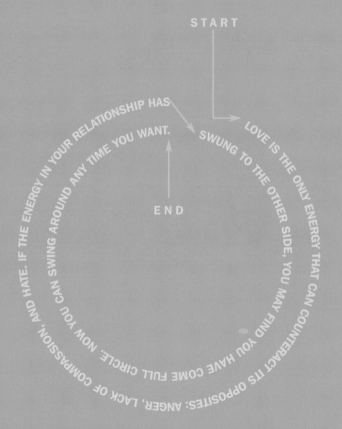

START

LOVE IS THE ONLY ENERGY THAT CAN COUNTERACT ITS OPPOSITES: ANGER, LACK OF COMPASSION, AND HATE. IF THE ENERGY IN YOUR RELATIONSHIP HAS SWUNG TO THE OTHER SIDE, YOU MAY FIND YOU HAVE COME FULL CIRCLE. NOW YOU CAN SWING AROUND ANY TIME YOU WANT.

END

DO YOU LOVE YOURSELF ENOUGH TO RISK SUCCESS?

THE LOVE YOU ARE
SEEKING IS THE LOVE YOU
DESERVE TO HAVE.

Respect for others is manifested by your manners and the energy you project. It can be hard to show respect for someone, especially when they're not behaving in a respectful or loving way towards you. But if you stay with it (do try!), you'll eventually transcend any feelings that are not love-based.

Your heart is the great processor of all higher and lower energies. Your approach will be unbalanced if your energy is either too physical or too intellectual. The heart is there to mediate, to purify, and neutralize the extreme energies that are entering the fray!

LISTEN to your heart's desires. Your heart is the key to

HEAD + HEART

unlocking their expression. Even when it seems illogical,

= GROWTH

your heart leads you to exactly where you should be.

OF THE SOUL

Continuous positive thoughts generate love. Continuous negative thoughts generate its opposite. Thought is energy and how we think is the way we create. Energy has duality: thoughts can be positive, showing love, joy, and compassion; or negative, showing fear, anger, and hatred.

Check your inner dialogue: is your energy currently up or down?

Love can soften all the rough edges in your mind, body, and spirit. As the life force of the Universe it's the cosmic superglue that holds everything together. Next time you're facing a choice between love and money or material things, remember to go for the thing that is priceless.

It happens: someone
          declares their affections
for you or professes their
          deepest love and all of a
sudden you feel as though
    you're having an out-of-body
experience. You've lifted off!
          And when you come back
down to earth you want to
          know whether they truly
mean what they're saying.
          The only way to know for
sure is to listen to your
          heart. Your heart knows
when it's for real.

RELAX!

There will always be another chance. If you have let something pass you by because you felt fearful or unready, the Universe will design another opportunity for you to finally step up and get it right. So don't panic or beat yourself up. There will be a second, third or fourth chance in the future. RELAX!

Love that is taken for granted is love on a time limit.

Love needs flexibility but it can't be endlessly pushed. Love that is taken for granted is love on a time limit.

Your current relationship situation is exactly what you have created. The Universe has simply handed back to you that which you have focused on. If things are not as you would have them you need to create something new! Your belief system is the key. Examine your deeply held beliefs. Do you honestly believe you are lovable in every respect? Do you think you deserve the love and passion that you crave? You have to believe it to make it happen. So think again.

FIND LOVE, JOY, AND HAPPINESS IN THE LITTLE THINGS. A GREAT LOVE LIFE IS THE SAME AS HAVING A GREAT LOVE OF LIFE. BE ONE OF THE JOYFUL. LOVE IS WITHIN AND AROUND YOU ALWAYS.

Are you a lover or a fighter?

You have acted with courage and integrity. And that is all that is required of you in any situation. You have allowed your heart to be clear and you have honored its message. You have faith in yourself. Now you are free to go!

HAVE A
CHANGE OF
HEART.
CHANGE YOUR
ATTITUDE TO
LOVE.

Your love connections are in a state

of transition and you are beginning

to see where true depth lies.

Following this leads you to the right

place for your highest learning.

The love that is eluding you is simply a message directly from the Universe. You are capable of having ALL the love you desire but for some reason you are endorsing a mentality of lack instead. You came from love originally—as did all humanity —but your fears and insecurities will keep you from having the love you are worthy of. If you are love, how can you not have it? Agree to be worthy.

MAKE LOVE YOUR HIGHEST GOAL
AND YOU WILL SEE WHERE AND
HOW IT SHOWS UP IN YOUR LIFE.

Unconditional love is the love you have for others, irrespective of their flaws (maybe even because of them!). The flaws you see in others are flaws you have recognized in yourself. They may not be a part of you right now, but you have recognized them so you can accept them too.

Love is everywhere. ✳

LOVE NEEDS FLEXIBILITY BUT IT

CAN'T BE ENDLESSLY PUSHED.

LOVE THAT IS TAKEN FOR

GRANTED IS LOVE ON A TIME LIMIT.

LOVE IS MIND OVER MATTER.

Trying to control the flow of love is like controlling a puppet—it's too conditional on what you do to keep it there. What happens if you stop holding the strings? You just have to love and let live. This means letting go and seeing what love really does when left to its own devices, which, by the way, are infinite!

TRUTH

COMMUNICATION

EXPRESSION

SILENCE

DIALOGUE

EMOTIONS (SPOKEN

VERSUS UNSPOKEN)

UNDERSTANDING

HONESTY

CLOSURE

TRUTH

[throat chakra]

Watch. Wait. Feel the answer rather than talk until you get one. Sometimes talking clouds an issue. See what comes up when you don't go there! If it's clarity you're seeking, try turning off and tuning into the energies instead. Then let the answer come out of the silence.

You
already
know the
truth.
You just
have to
allow it.

"The ultimate mind-altering drug is truth.

Lily Tomlin

YOUR WORDS ARE YOUR LEGACY. YOU

CAN CHANGE YOUR MIND AND EXPRESS

ANOTHER INTENTION OR MAKE ANOTHER

DECISION. HOWEVER, IF YOU SAY YOU'RE

GOING TO DO SOMETHING, DO IT. FOR

GOD'S SAKE. AND YOURS TOO.

If it's frustration or anger you're temporarily experiencing, let it be just that—a temporary, if intense, experience. Process it however you can.

The REAL game of life

To give as good as you get is not a goal in the game of life. Just because someone gives you a serve doesn't mean you have to turn around and whack the ball straight back in their face. You can let a few slip by, you know! Pick wisely which ones you'll return and you'll be much more effective. You'll be in charge, too, as you're no longer on the defensive.

Anyone who has done the wrong thing by you will either already know or will eventually come to realize. Recognize this and you'll be released from the need to be upset or angry. Nor should you feel the need for any sort of vengeance. Let the Universe take care of it for you. And move on.

The consequences of not speaking your truth will almost always be worse than your fear of doing so.

YOUR CLEAR VIEW ON THINGS MAY LEAD YOU TO SPEAK WITHOUT ANY HEED TO WHO MAY BE LISTENING. BE CERTAIN THAT WHOEVER YOU COMMUNICATE YOUR VIEW TO IS READY TO HEAR IT IN SUCH DIRECT TERMS. SOMETIMES IT'S KINDER (AND SAFER) TO GO SOFTLY. YOU CAN STILL DELIVER THE MESSAGE.

Insight is gained from experience. Since you've been gaining a bit lately you have all the necessary powers of discrimination to tell it how it really is. You're hitting your mark with freaky accuracy. This gives you a new confidence. Suddenly you're the girl everyone wants to talk to!

SPEAK YOUR MIND.

LEAVE FEAR BEHIND.

The spotlight of judgment is firmly focused on you at the moment. Why? Because you've been down on yourself and now the external world has shifted accordingly. The criticism may be difficult to hear, but try anyway. You never know, there may be more than a grain of truth in it. Try not to take it too personally. If it can help you in any way it's all good!

Emotional honesty is hard for someone you are close to. Coax them gently by letting them know they are safe to express intimate things to you. Reassure them that you will not hold them to it; nor will you judge them for their effort. Let them know that your turn will come.

HEAR WHAT YOU DON'T WANT TO HEAR. SAY WHAT YOU DON'T WANT TO SAY. GO WHERE YOU DON'T WANT TO GO. PUSH YOURSELF.

HUMOR IS THE BEST WEAPON YOU HAVE. DEFLECT WHATEVER YOU KNOW IS NOT FOR REAL WITH A SMILE AND A JOKE. BECAUSE WHATEVER GOES ON AND NO MATTER WHO SAYS WHAT, WHEN PEOPLE TAKE IT TOO SERIOUSLY IT'S FUNNY! SO YOU CAN AFFORD TO LAUGH OUT LOUD. THE UNIVERSE IS ONLY TRYING TO TEASE YOU INTO A REACTION.

IF SOMEONE IS

DELIBERATELY WITHHOLDING

OR NOT EXPRESSING

THEIR EMOTIONS RESPECT THEIR

RIGHT TO DO SO.

YOU MAY NOT THINK IT'S

HEALTHY (AND IT MAY NOT BE)

BUT THEY ARE ON THEIR

PATH TOO.

You demand what you want and it feels good. This is a wonderful time in your life when you refuse to be held back or down. When you assert yourself in this way you set the pace for everyone else. Respect is the unintended by-product of having the courage to go for it. And as the saying goes, no guts—no glory!

If you hear a constant stream of negativity it will change the way you think—about yourself, about others, about life. Honor yourself so you're not polluted by someone else's baggage. Be on the lookout for anyone who's heavily into negative dialogue. Be vigilant whenever you think it's about to start. It's not healthy.

Block your ears!

closure

Closure: that old chestnut! No one can tell you how to get closure. Whether it's the end of a certain chapter in your life, a relationship, a friendship, gone awry, or you're leaving a place you have lived in for years, closure is situation-specific. There's no time frame that absolutely works and there's no formula for how it should happen. You'll have to figure out what is best for you.

IF SOMEONE TELLS YOU SOMETHING THAT IS PAINFUL TO HEAR, TAKE THE POSITION THAT THEY ARE DOING IT BECAUSE THEY CARE ABOUT YOU. THIS WILL ALLOW YOU TO BE COMPASSIONATE TOWARDS THEM. THEN YOU CAN RECEIVE WHATEVER IT IS THEY ARE SAYING WITHOUT RESENTMENT. LISTENING TO SOMEONE IS USUALLY MORE IMPORTANT THAN AGREEING WITH THEM.

If you were ever tempted to lie about your feelings, think about this: the moment you do, you set up circumstances that will come back to bite you eventually. Be open, honest and clear in your communication. The joy of being fully and totally understood is the reward of proper communication. You are giving and receiving in equal measure. Your ability to listen and respond leads to a real connection that lasts.

Whatever you've had on your mind lately is about to explode from the depths to the surface. If you're unwilling to be up-front right now, perhaps it's because you don't feel you can really say what you think. To issue an effective piece of communication your delivery must be calm, considered, and compassionate. If you're in Krakatoa mode, for heaven's sake speak to someone else first to reduce the risk of eruption! Release the pressure!

Sorry

If you have any regrets about anything, let yourself off the hook. "I'M SORRY" and "PLEASE FORGIVE ME" are essential phrases to have in your handbook. Don't leave home without them.

Once you've said it, let it go.

IF SOMETHING YOU'VE SAID HAS MADE YOU FEEL AS THOUGH YOU'VE STUFFED UP BIG TIME, THERE'S ONLY ONE WAY YOU CAN GO: FORWARD. MEND AND REPAIR WHEREVER YOU CAN. HOWEVER, IF MAJOR DAMAGE HAS BEEN DONE YOU'LL JUST HAVE TO TAKE RESPONSIBILITY AND WEAR IT. THAT'S YOUR LESSON. OVER TIME YOU'LL BE BETTER ABLE TO WORK OUT WHAT WENT WRONG AND WHY THINGS TURNED OUT THE WAY THEY DID.

Practice random thoughts of kindness!

Speak kindly to yourself and you'll have no trouble doing the same for everyone.

DECISIONS

TURNING POINTS

PATH

PERCEPTION

PSYCHIC QUALITIES

DREAMS

CONCENTRATION

FOCUS

ENLIGHTENMENT

INTUITION

AWARENESS

CROSSROADS

[third eye chakra]

170

destiny

Choice gives you power. Power gives you grace. Grace gives you awareness. And awareness gives you your destiny.

DON'T HESITATE.

A turning point on any spiritual or personal journey usually presents as a particularly intense experience, and often it will have unintended or prolonged effects. The only thing that can help you understand it is time and a different viewing platform. Bear in mind that we're not always meant to understand everything at the time at which it occurs (or doesn't). That's a lesson in itself.

LOSS

LOSS IS THE NATURAL SUCCESSOR TO ATTACHMENT. IF LIFE IS A SERIES OF ATTACHMENTS, THEN LOSS IS THE CORNERSTONE OF LIFE'S ULTIMATE TEST. THROUGH LOSING SOMETHING WE ARE FORCED TO RECOGNIZE OUR OWN LIMITLESSNESS, OUR ETERNAL NATURE IN THE SPIRITUAL REALM, AND OUR FINITE NATURE IN THE PHYSICAL. ABUNDANCE IS OUR NATURAL STATE AND IT IS ONLY OUR MIND THAT DWELLS ON WHAT HAS BEEN LET GO OF OR LOST. THE SOUL KNOWS WHAT WE NEED TO EXPERIENCE.

patience

WAITING IS NOT ON! Patience is, but waiting and patience are not always the same thing. Recognize the difference. Your life is not waiting for you to play catch up. It's on right now! Don't allow anyone else to fool you into waiting either. That's their agenda, not yours. Know when you're on hold and when you really need to exercise patience. Wait only when you're ahead of the curve (and when you can afford to be patient) and not when you're behind it.

BLINK AND YOU
CAN MISS IT.
SHUT YOUR EYES AND
YOU'LL NEVER SEE IT.

Sometimes the calm before the storm is for relief rather than a warning. You can opt not to buy into the tension and instead use the space to prepare for what's coming. Get set. Get what's coming.

THE CRITICAL MOMENT LEADS YOU TO A NEW
PLACE ON THE JOURNEY. OFTEN WHERE YOU END UP
LOOKS NOTHING LIKE THE PLACE YOU ENVISAGED.
BUT ON CLOSER INSPECTION IT WILL CONTAIN THE
ELEMENTS OF EVERYTHING YOU NEED.

Don't snatch defeat from the jaws of victory. Choose your next move carefully, at the time that feels right for you.

Random events can appear to be unsettling. They are designed to be that way, to keep you on your toes and (believe it or not) to keep you interested. Don't panic. Rise to the challenge. It could be your personal Olympics!

EXPECT IT. WATCH IT HAPPEN.

Sometimes you have to compromise in order to help yourself. The time for such a course of action will be obvious. Either the circumstances will demand it or you'll be forced to by other unforseen factors. The outcome may even look like it goes against you. But this is a test of faith to see whether you can back your intuition and act in a way that is ultimately for the highest good of all concerned.

Celebrate all your changes to date. You have learned many lessons well and the Universe urges you to honor the changes you have undergone. You have acted with integrity, belief, and faith. This is what you were meant to do. And what you have pulled off is a reinvention of your SELF. You have come through the chrysalis phase of your life. Congratulations.

enter the butterfly!

dream

As you sleep you are constantly dreaming. But you won't recall all your dreams all the time. Your dreams provide clues to your next step and are potential destiny points just waiting to be noticed. So write them down upon awakening. Even if there are symbols, scenes or conversations that you can't quite remember, there may be just enough detail for you to make sense of. The messages are struggling to be received. Remember: as a dreamer, you never really sleep.

ACTIONS

+

RISK

=

REWARD

Your personal routine is possibly getting a little stale. Consider the possibility of a revamp in your daily life. Doors may be opening to you, offering a variety of fresh opportunities for change. If you ignore them or you don't enter them now you run the risk they'll have closed when you think you're finally ready.

THERE IS ANOTHER WAY OF LOOKING AT THE SITUATION AT HAND.

BEFORE YOU IMPULSIVELY JUMP INTO THE COMPLICATIONS, LOOK

FOR—AND FEEL—THE SIMPLE ANSWER. THE INFORMATION YOU

HAVE GATHERED DOESN'T REFLECT THE REALITY AT ALL. IT'S THE

CLOUDY STUFF OBSCURING THE CORE ISSUES.

Your ship is about to come in! When it does, be ready for it. Prepare and get organized as soon as possible. Anything outstanding needs to be resolved. Attend to the details of your life, no matter how tedious the task seems. When your instinct is to start stripping down to the essentials or to get closure on things you'll know you're entering a new phase. If you feel the need to throw out your old clothes, photographs, memorabilia or your worldly goods, it's a sign things are changing. Honor it. You won't regret it.

SEEK CLARITY. GAIN CONSCIOUSNESS. PUSH THROUGH THE BARRIERS OF YOUR OWN EXISTENCE. AND EXPERIENCE A HIGHER POWER.

Life has a way of shaking you up to test your faith. Sometimes you go through a period of what seems like non-stop carnage, when no matter what you do nothing goes right. Things look like (and may be) a complete disaster. And that's okay (really!). Don't be too hard on yourself. It's how you react to what's going down that's critical now. Do you totally fold or do you dust yourself off to muscle through another round? You know you'll come out the other end eventually. Now it's over to you.

BELIEVE IT.
PERCEIVE IT.
RECEIVE IT.
AND DETACH.

Meditation

Meditation is the ultimate place of learning. It's not a cop-out to do nothing. That's exactly the point! When you meditate you are simply allowing yourself to be. Suspended in peace, you just exist. You are thought-less. Weight-less. Perfect. Concentration takes you deeper. You are being pulled within for a reason. You are reminded of who you really are, beneath the persona you present to the world at large. Lose your mind and find yourself.

The way in is the only real way out

Perception is your front-line tool in managing the internal and external environment. When you train yourself to perceive everything around you and inside you, even the most tiny of details, you'll start to see how these elements add up to a far greater whole. And rather than being caught up in distractions and noise you'll become aware of the many subtle layers of being alive.

You go, Amazon g

192

You have reached a point where you accurately perceive your own strengths and weaknesses. No longer are you fearful of finding anything out about yourself. Not for you the false protection of self-deception! You welcome it all—the good, the bad or the ugly—because you can. By focusing on your strengths, anything else just falls away.

You go, Amazon girl!

ENLIGHTENMENT AND AWARENESS ARE YOUR
GOALS. PATIENCE AND PERSEVERANCE ARE YOUR
TOOLS. DISCIPLINE AND INTUITION ARE YOUR
ALLIES. DECIDE THE SACRIFICES YOU'RE WILLING
TO MAKE IN PURSUIT OF THE DESIRES YOU HAVE.
WHAT DECISIONS YOU MAKE WILL DETERMINE THE
FLOW. THE THINGS YOU'RE WILLING TO
FOREGO WILL BE IN PROPORTION TO THE
OUTCOME YOU'RE SEEKING.

YOU ARE NOT AFRAID OF YOUR DECISIONS. YOU ACCEPT THAT FREE WILL IS YOUR BACK-UP TO ANY DECISION YOU TAKE. YOU CAN CHANGE YOUR MIND AT ANY TIME AND CHOOSE ANOTHER DECISION.

TAKE A BREATH.

TAKE YOUR TIME.

TAKE CONTROL.

DESTINY

THE UNIVERSE

CONSCIOUSNESS

CONNECTION

DIRECTION

PERSONAL PURPOSE

UNITY

HOLISTIC

GREATER GOOD

DESTINY

[crown chakra]

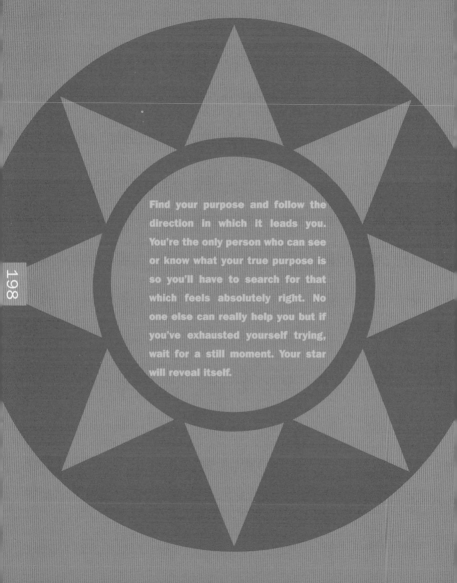

Find your purpose and follow the direction in which it leads you. You're the only person who can see or know what your true purpose is so you'll have to search for that which feels absolutely right. No one else can really help you but if you've exhausted yourself trying, wait for a still moment. Your star will reveal itself.

Dig deep

If, as is said, the whole Universe is contained in a flower or in a grain of sand, then it is also contained in you. You have all the resources within you that you need.

When you focus
on what is unique
about every
person in your life
and every person
you come into
contact with, you
can see the light
that is common to
us all.

YOU MUST BE WILLING TO DO THE WORK.

How many times do you have to hear something before you believe it? On the other hand, how many times do words have nothing behind them and how often do you fall into their abyss? You knew all along that you're capable of perceiving the true destiny of every situation that you come across. Don't doubt it. Don't doubt yourself.

CONTINUE TO BECOME YOURSELF.
ABOVE ANYONE ELSE.

HOLD OUT FOR THE BEST.

JUST BECAUSE THINGS MAY NOT LOOK
LIKE THEY'RE WORKING OUT (FOR YOU), IT
DOESN'T MEAN THEY'RE NOT! YOU COULD
BE RIGHT ON TRACK. WHAT LOOKS AT
FIRST GLANCE TO BE A DISASTER FOR YOU
COULD BE THE GREATEST BLESSING OF
ALL. AND THE ONE THAT PROPELS YOU TO
A HIGHER PLACE.

As an individual, you have the right to express your unique purpose in any way you choose. As long as you do! Your beat is unlike anyone else's so dance to the rhythm that serves your highest good. No one should be able to trip you up. If they can, you weren't commited sufficiently to it.

Let them try!

THERE WILL BE PEOPLE ON YOUR PATH YOU ARE

DESTINED TO MEET. THEY ARE HELPERS WHO, IN LINE

WITH THEIR OWN DESTINY AND PURPOSE, WILL

INTERSECT WITH YOU SO EACH OF YOU CAN FULFILL

YOUR MISSIONS. THESE HELPERS ARE VITAL AND YOU

NEED TO ALLOW THEM TO PLAY THEIR ROLE. THEY ARE

YOUR TEACHERS, AS YOU ARE THEIRS.

208

Essential for your destiny is a unified and holistic approach. In other words, girls, it's a mind-body-spirit gig. There's no getting around it.

YOU can't tackle anything from just one angle and expect a coherent result.

peace

YOU WILL FIND PEACE OF MIND WHEN YOU HAVE PEACE IN MIND

miracle

The miracle is not only that you have a unique destiny, but that you are uniquely suited to it.

THE DIRECTION YOU TAKE IN LIFE IS A FUNCTION OF HOW WELL YOU USE THE OPPORTUNITIES AND EXPERIENCES YOU HAVE IN FRONT OF YOU. THAT'S WHY A SEEMINGLY DEAD-END JOB CAN GIVE YOU ALL THE THINGS YOU NEED TO ACCOMPLISH SOMETHING VERY EXCITING IN THE LONG TERM. IT CAN SHOW YOU THE MEANING OF TENACITY AND PERSEVERANCE. IT CAN ALSO TEACH YOU COMPASSION, SO THAT WHEN YOU MOVE ON TO SOMETHING BIGGER OR BETTER, YOU'LL HAVE COMPASSION FOR OTHERS WHO HOLD DOWN SMALLER JOBS, KNOWING THAT THEY HAVE THEIR DESTINY TOO.

THE
INFINITE
INTELLIGENCE
COUNTS YOU AMONG
ITS VAST RESOURCES.
UNDERSTAND THAT
YOU ARE AN ASSET TO
THE UNIVERSE. KNOW
THIS AND YOU'LL
ACHIEVE ALL THAT
YOU SET OUT
TO.

The connection between all of us means that we each have to take our share of responsibility for all the things that happen in life. Whether it's a tragedy in a country on the other side of the world or the beauty of a new galaxy being revealed to scientists, we are connected to it. You can't share in the beauty without also owning the flipside.

VOLUNTEER FOR LIFE. GIVE OF YOURSELF TO OTHERS WHO NEED IT.

WHEN YOU ACT IN THE INTERESTS OF THE GREATER GOOD YOU ARE SHOWING A GENEROSITY OF SPIRIT AND A HIGHER CONSCIOUSNESS THAT IS NEVER IGNORED BY THE UNIVERSE. PROVIDING YOUR SERVICE IN LIFE TO IMPROVE IT IN SOME WAY WILL BRING YOU SUCCESS. IT'S ABOUT LEAVING THINGS BETTER THAN YOU FOUND THEM.

in
sync.

You are plugged into the energy of higher consciousness and you are able to operate with a clarity that is truly stunning. This is your ability now: to cut through to the essence of all things that you come across. You are in sync.

TODAY YOU HAVE THE POWER TO RENEW YOURSELF. ONLY BY THROWING OFF THE PAST CAN YOU RE-ALIGN YOURSELF WITH YOUR DESTINY. ALL THAT COUNTS IS WHAT YOU CAN BRING WITH YOU TO CAPITALIZE ON FOR YOUR FUTURE. SO IF YOU ONLY HAVE ONE STRENGTH BUT YOU HAVE 100 WEAKNESSES FOCUS ON THAT ONE STRENGTH UNTIL YOU HAVE 100 STRENGTHS AND ONE WEAKNESS. THIS IS HOW YOU ELEVATE YOURSELF.

Your imagination is limitless but you may not be allowing it to have its head! Use what you've been given: a beautiful internal world that YOU alone can design and control! Your creativity can be a tool for consciousness. Let the cosmos show you what you can do while you're here. Turn on, tune in, and go all out!

THE WISDOM YOU SEEK IS AVAILABLE TO YOU AT ANY TIME YOU NEED IT.

Living in line with your destiny means that you're moving towards freedom. If, as you progress, you find you're feeling more trapped and less able to do or go where you want, it's a sure sign you're getting off the track. And if you're straying from your path, the right things or people will not be able to come to you.

You are a

free spirit.

But being a free spirit comes with responsibilities. You must honor your responsibilities and be free with your heart at the same time.

If you feel the need to change your situation, do it sooner rather than later. The Universe is patient but what begins with a whisper of destiny's calling will end up being an ear-splitting roar if you ignore it. Ignoring the call can only result in one thing: you'll end up having to make the change anyway, but by the time you do, it will be a giant headache!

You will awaken to the many layers of higher consciousness by refusing to be disillusioned by anything that happens in your life. There is nothing that occurs that is without karmic reason. Always remember that you are a part of the divine plan.